TAKE
Courage!

COMPANION JOURNAL
BY LINDA SMITH, BS AND MARY BETH WOLL, MA, LMHC

All Scriptures are quoted from the New International Version.

©2024 The Widows Project

All rights reserved. No portion of this book may be reproduced, stored in a retrieval system, or transmitted in any form or by any means—electronic, mechanical, photocopy, recording, scanning or other—except for brief quotations in critical reviews or articles, without the prior written permission of the authors.

ISBN paperback: **978-1-7362169-7-2**

David Woll: Cover Design
Kristi Knowles: Interior Layout/Design

Take Courage Journal Introduction

Take Courage has a very definite purpose and goal—to offer you healing support during your grieving process.

We want to help you recover from your devastating loss so you can move forward into a life of effectiveness for God, becoming fruitful; even 30, 60, and 100 times more productive than you ever were before! (Mark 4:20).

We have designed this journal to be used as a companion to Take Courage! Growing Stronger After Losing Your Spouse. Each chapter has a recovery focus with an accompanying life principle and Scripture.

How to use this journal:

Each week, as you prepare for and meet with your Take Courage group, we have provided space in your journal for

1. *Study notes,*
2. *Meeting notes, and*
3. *Reflections.*

These authors wrote this book and journal because we all care about you! We have been where you are now. We pray that God will bless you with His love and comfort as you grow stronger through your Take Courage journey.

With love and prayers,

Mary Beth and *Linda*

Mary Beth Woll, MA, LMHC
Linda Smith, BS

Chapter 1

Is it Okay to Cry?

Allow your soul to find rest by crying.

*"Weeping may endure for a night,
but joy comes in the morning" (Psalm 30:5).*

Study Notes

Further Reflection

Chapter 2
I Forgive

By forgiving, I take responsibility for my own reactions.

*"In this world you will have trouble. But take heart!
I have overcome the world" (John 16:33).*

Study Notes

Meeting Notes

Further Reflection

Chapter 3

Fear Not!

When we are afraid, God will provide the help we need.

*"Fear not, for I am with you; do not be dismayed,
for I am your God. I will strengthen you and help you. I will
uphold you with My righteous right hand" (Isaiah 41:10).*

Study Notes

Meeting Notes

Further Reflection

CHAPTER 4

SING WHEN YOU CAN'T UNDERSTAND

God is with me in my emotional highs and lows and everywhere in between.

"And we know that in all things God works for the good of those who love Him, who have been called according to His purpose" (Romans 8:28).

Study Notes

Meeting Notes

Further Reflection

Chapter 5

Pray, Pray, Pray!

In every season, God will hear and answer my cries for help.

"Rejoice always, pray continually, give thanks in all circumstance, for this is God's will for you in Christ Jesus"
(I Thessalonians 5:16-18).

Study Notes

Meeting Notes

Further Reflection

Chapter 6

Caring for Yourself, the Widowed

As you gain skills in organizing, your confidence that you can indeed bring order out of chaos will grow.

"'For I know the plans I have for you,' declares the Lord, 'plans to prosper you and not to harm you, plans to give you hope and a future'" (Jeremiah 29:11).

Study Notes

Meeting Notes

Further Reflection

Chapter 7

WHAT NOW? FINDING PURPOSE IN, DURING, AND AFTER THE LOSS

My life's purpose did not end when my beloved husband died.

"The Lord will fulfill His purpose for me; Your steadfast love, O Lord, endures forever. Do not forsake the work of Your hands"
(Psalm 138:8, ESV).

Study Notes

Meeting Notes

Further Reflection

Chapter 8

Rebuild

In order to rebuild, we grieve each secondary loss to God.

"And the God of all grace who called you to His eternal glory in Christ, after you have suffered a little while, will Himself restore you and make you strong, firm, and steadfast" (I Peter 5:10).

Study Notes

Meeting Notes

Further Reflection

CHAPTER 9

MOVING FORWARD

I still have a purpose for living!

"You did not choose Me, but I chose you and appointed you to go and bear fruit, fruit that will last" (John 15:16).

Study Notes

Meeting Notes

Further Reflection

Chapter 10

Complicated Grief

I can overcome complicated grief by telling my story, receiving support from the Body of Christ, and pursuing counsel.

"The Lord is close to the brokenhearted and saves those who are crushed in spirit" (Psalm 34:18).

Study Notes

Meeting Notes

Further Reflection

CHAPTER 11

WIDOWED PARENTING:
TIPS FOR PARENTING AFTER LOSS

*Being supportive, not perfect, is the goal
of helping our kids through their loss.*

*"Praise be to the God and Father of our Lord Jesus Christ,
the Father of compassion and the God of all comfort,
Who comforts us in all our troubles, so that we can comfort
those in any trouble with the comfort we ourselves have
received from God" (2 Corinthian 1:3-40).*

Study Notes

Further Reflection

CHAPTER 12

MY NEW IDENTITY

My spouse is gone, so now God will help me build a new life.

"The life I now live in the body, I live by faith in the Son of God, who loved me and gave Himself for me" (Galatians 2:20b).

Study Notes

Meeting Notes

Further Reflection

www.ingramcontent.com/pod-product-compliance
Lightning Source LLC
Chambersburg PA
CBHW061740070526
44585CB00024B/2752